napkins

napkins

*the art of folding,
adorning and embellishing*

Andrea Spencer

photography by Spike Powell

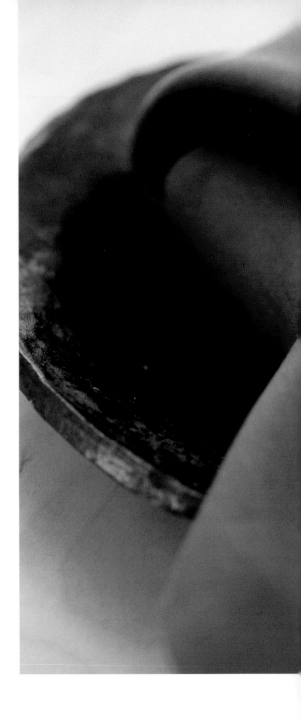

I would like to thank Spike Powell for taking such beautiful
pictures, Joanne Rippin for her support and patience, and
Tessa Eveleigh for writing the text. Thanks also to the
following for so very kindly loaning me accessories and
napkins for the book. The Dining Room Shop, 62-64 White
Hart Lane, London SW13 OPZ, Tel: 020 8878 1020;
Pimpernel & Partners, 596 Kings Road, London SW6 2DX,
Tel: 020 7731 2448; Decorative Living, 55 New Kings Road,
London SW6, Tel: 020 7736 5623; Divertimenti, 139-41
Fulham Road, London SW3, Tel: 020 7581 8065; Nicole
Fabre, 592 Kings Road, London SW6 2DX, Tel: 020 7384
3112; Le Jacquard Francais, Tel: 01225 466062; VV Rouleaux,
54 Sloane Square, London SW1 8AX, Tel: 020 7730 3125;
Heal's, 196 Tottenham Court Road, London W1P 9LD and
also The Cafe at Heal's for allowing us to photograph in the
restaurant; Tobias and the Angel, 68 White Hart Lane,
London SW13 OPZ, Tel: 020 8878 8902; Myriad Antiques,
131 Portland Road, London W11 4LW, Tel: 020 7229 1709.

This edition is published by Aquamarine,
an imprint of Anness Publishing Ltd, Blaby Road, Wigston,
Leicestershire LE18 4SE; info@anness.com

www.aquamarinebooks.com; www.annesspublishing.com

If you like the images in this book and would like to
investigate using them for publishing, promotions
or advertising, please visit our website
www.practicalpictures.com for more information.

Publisher Joanna Lorenz
Managing Editor Helen Sudell
Senior Editor Joanne Rippin
Text written by Tessa Evelegh
Classic fold designs supplied by Paul Jackson
Illustrations Lucinda Ganderton
Production Controller Ann Childers

A CIP catalogue record for this book is available from
the British Library.

PUBLISHER'S NOTE
Although the advice and information in this book are
believed to be accurate and true at the time of going to
press, neither the authors nor the publisher can accept any
legal responsibility or liability for any errors or omissions that
may have been made nor for any inaccuracies nor for any
loss, harm or injury that comes about from following
instructions or advice in this book.

contents

6   Introduction

8   Napery, past and present

16   Napkins for Occasions

32   Decorated Napkins

46   Holding and Folding

72   Napkin Rings

86   Napkin Themes

104   Classical Napkin Folds

140   Stitch Directory

142   Napkin Folding Symbols

143   Templates

144   Index

introduction

Whether you are planning a formal dinner or a simple picnic, the table will set the scene, creating a sense of anticipation among the guests for a special time together. While we would all love the opportunity to start from scratch for each occasion, this is not viable. In reality few of us have the finances, let alone storage space, for endless sets of china and glass that cater for every entertaining event. The best solution is to concentrate on detail. You really can create completely different looks and moods simply by changing the accessories. A table dressed for dinner in crisp white linen and best china, then accessorized with sparkling cut glass, flickering candles and exotically folded napkins, immediately sets the mood for a formal occasion, perhaps a special celebration. On another occasion simply change the napkins to an extrovert lime green, either folded at each place, or tucked into brightly-coloured napkin rings, and guests will immediately anticipate an altogether more informal and relaxed affair.

The key is to invest in some classic china, glass and cutlery that you know you will love for years to come. Use these as the main ingredients for every table setting, and dress them up or down to create the right ambience for each occasion. Candles and flowers, with their natural seasonal variety, have always been a quick way to make a change, but of all the more permanent elements of table setting, the easiest and most cost effective to change or adapt are the linens.

There are two routes to follow when choosing napkins. The first is to invest in some exquisite white or cream linen dinner napkins, alternatively cotton damask. Linens have a quality that will last a lifetime or longer, as they can be handed down from generation to generation. Freshly laundered, they always look wonderful, and years of hot washing and starching gives linens and heavy cottons a glorious appearance and feel that goes on improving with age. A set of fine linen napkins is always a marvellous present, and you could scour antique markets and pick up some Victorian originals that will still have plenty of life in them. They will look wonderful on the table, even if you just press them and fold them simply. Napkins can also be dressed up or down to suit each occasion with ribbon ties, coloured napkin rings, or even flowers from the garden. For more formal occasions, you could experiment with some of the more elaborate classic napkin folds.

The other route to follow with napkins, and there is no reason why you should not follow both routes for ultimate flexibility, is to pick up contemporary napkins in the latest shades and designs from the more fashionable high-street interiors stores. For less than the cost of a vase of flowers, you can invest in a set of napkins which will instantly change the look of your table. Added to your classic tableware basics, they will give your table settings a whole new slant. You will find you can transform the look of your table further by adapting or changing the napkins' folds or shape, or by adding some simple decoration.

Packed within the pages of this book are a host of creative ways to use napkins for widely different table-setting themes. You can discover how to fold, knot, wrap, embroider and decorate them, as well as making napkin rings out of everything from beaded wire and safety pins, to paper and tin foil. This delightful array of designs and inspirational ideas, so beautifully presented, will transform the way you think of napkins, and will add a new dimension to your meal times.

Top left Bamboo-handled cutlery, a lacquer-red bowl and the woven plate underneath, give this setting an Oriental feel that is emphasized by the tassel on the napkin. **Top right** Sprigs of spring herbs lend a fresh feel to a simple organdie napkin. **Bottom left** Napkins can be used to line bowls for a table decoration. **Bottom right** Where breezy weather threatens to blow away the napkins, use pebbles from the beach to hold them down.

napery, past and present

Unheard of before the Middle Ages napkins had, by the 17th century, become status symbols. When napkins were at their most popular a complex code of etiquette surrounded their usage, which thankfully has become much simpler in the 21st century – as has the painstaking laundry which was also once required.

napkins through the ages

There's something so satisfying about the look and feel of crisp, freshly laundered white linen that it has endured as the favourite table covering for hundreds of years. Napkins are the individual element of table linens; one for each diner to protect their clothes from spills and stains, and to use to dab clean lips and fingertips. In fact, napkins used to be a part of the tablecloth itself, and the word napkin comes directly from *nape*, the French for tablecloth.

Unheard of in Europe until the Middle Ages, there was clearly a need for napkins at that time. Table cutlery was not widely used, and people ate with their hands, which they then wiped clean on a part of the tablecloth. As each course was finished, so a messy debris of food built up and the cloth had to be changed. The French developed the idea of adding an extra cover to the edge of the table. This was easily detachable, and so could be exchanged for a clean one partway through the meal without having to clear the tabletop completely. A small charge to recoup laundry costs was made for each 'cover', and the term is still used in some restaurants today to indicate the number of diners at the table. It was not long before these covers became permanently detached from the tablecloth and were used as the napkins we know today.

By the beginning of the 17th century, the then fashionable neck ruffs meant napkins on the lap had become redundant. Protection from spills was needed much higher up, so napkins began to be tied around necks, becoming ever more generous as the ruffs became more flamboyant. Guests became responsible for their own napkins, and would fit the napkin to suit their ruff. Naturally, the larger the ruff, the larger the napkin had to be, and, over time, enormous napkins became an unlikely status symbol.

By the end of the 17th century, it was not just size that mattered; shape was important too. Napkins were folded into ever more ornate shapes. Fans, flowers, birds and even heraldic signs graced the smartest of tables. There were folds for gentlemen and even more elaborate folds for ladies. At really smart functions, each place was given an individual fold and the competition became so intense, that butlers were sent from London to Paris to perfect their folding skills.

With the Georgian era in the 18th century, dining took on a much more restrained look and napkin folding fell out of favour as it was considered altogether far too fussy. It was not until the mid-19th century, with the rise of the middle classes, that napkin

This 13th-century painting shows a royal banquet in Tarragona in 1228. The white cloth that covers the table would also have been used by the guests to wipe their hands and faces.

folding was resurrected. By the late Victorian and early Edwardian period, fancy foldings were regarded as a touch vulgar, as was the custom of putting napkins on the side plate – as you were seen to be showing off the fine china of your main plates. The First World War released many people from these social restraints and, nowadays, we are much more relaxed. Napkins can be placed on main plates, side plates, to the side or above a setting, tucked into glasses or used to wrap the cutlery.

What to use where

You cannot go wrong with clean white linen napkins. Freshly laundered and sweetly scented, they have been the correct choice for formal occasions since the 16th century. The finest napkins are made of silk damask – characterized by intricate designs incorporated into the weave – and introduced into Europe from Damascus by Crusaders in the 12th century.

Once it arrived in Europe, damask was used by local craftsmen in France, Flanders and Ireland, who adapted the design to linen and cotton. These remain the most popular choices for table napkins. Traditionally, a set of damask linens formed part of a young woman's dowry. The women in the family would help her embroider each one with her family's initial, and once she was betrothed, this would be joined by her fiancé's initial, which would be intertwined with hers to create a monogram.

Afternoon tea, which was popular through the 19th and early 20th centuries, was the occasion on which the smallest and prettiest napkins were brought out. Seen mainly as a ladies' occasion, afternoon-tea napkins were often made of delicate materials, such as fine lawn, exquisitely embroidered and measuring a tiny 20–30cm (8–12in) square. For the cocktail hour, which became popular early in the 20th century, fine finger napkins made of gossamer fabrics such as lace, organdie and fine cotton lawn, were handed out for catching drips from glasses and wiping fingers clean as the canapés were passed around.

The large white napkins used informally by this 19th century mother and her children, as they share a brioche, make a pleasing contrast with the elaborately patterned tablecloth that is typical of the period.

The general rule for napkins is: the less formal the occasion, the smaller and more decorated the napkin can be. Dinner napkins should be generously proportioned – and can even measure up to 1m (1 yard) square – and should be left folded in half so a double thickness can cover the lap. For less formal dinners, you can use smaller napkins, about 75cm (30in) square, but no smaller than 50cm (20in) square. However, for a buffet lunch napkins should be as generous as possible, as food on a plate that is held or balanced is prone to spill.

For most entertaining today, all-over patterns and solid colours can be used for all but the most formal of occasions. If you keep a selection of types of napkin you are bound to be able to fit the right style to the occasion, especially if you customize them with one of the many ideas in the book.

care of table linens

Since the main raison d'être of table linen is to catch spills, stain removal has always been the first step in laundering. Modern proprietary stain removers followed by a machine wash have made this easier, but there are still particular stains that require a little attention.

Candle wax: Scrape off any excess. Sandwich the stained area between two pieces of blotting paper or brown wrapping paper, then press using a warm, dry iron. The wax will melt and be absorbed by the paper.

Red wine: Red wine is best treated immediately. First, soak up the spill with a kitchen towel. Then either douse the red wine with white wine and the stain should disappear, or sprinkle on a thick layer of salt, to soak up the wine.

Spicy food: Start by trying a stain remover. If you are still left with a stain, soak white cloths in a solution of 15ml/1 tbsp bleach to 1 litre (1¾ pints) cold water. Launder as normal.

Scorch marks: The use of a hot iron to press napkins means they are vulnerable to scorch marks. Avoid this by ironing while still damp and by keeping the iron moving. If a napkin does become scorched, soak it in cold milk as soon as possible, or soak in a solution of 15ml/ 1 tbsp bleach to 1 litre (1¾ pints) cold water.

Washing

Linen is strong, largely shrink-resistant, and can be safely washed at 60°C (140°F), which effectively washes out most food stains. Densely woven white cottons can also be washed at 60°C (140°F), though looser weaves, coloureds and polyester mixes should be laundered at no more than 40°C (100°F).

Pressing

The key to getting the best from napkins is in the starching and pressing. A well-starched napkin holds its folds the best, and perfectionists will add traditional starch to the rinsing water. However you can achieve similar results by stretching the still-damp napkins into shape, then pressing them using spray starch and a non-steam iron on a hot setting. First, press on the reverse side to avoid any watermarks and to remove most of the creases, then on the right side, to enhance the natural sheen.

Storing

In the old days, linens were stored in airing cupboards with slatted shelves to allow plenty of ventilation and prevent mildew and damp. They were also often scented with lavender, which is a natural antiseptic and insect repellent. Nowadays, with central heating, our houses are much drier, so linens can safely be kept in drawers and cupboards with solid shelves. Few of us have time to make scented lavender bags but the modern alternative is to use scented ironing water and then to line drawers with scented drawer liners.

dining out

Even nowadays, there is still an elaborate etiquette in the top hotels and restaurants around the world, where formal dinners and banquets are likely to be held. The first stumbling block is when to unfold the napkin. The waiters often deal with this: once everyone is seated they may go around the table, unfolding the napkins, then either handing them to each guest or flicking them into their laps. If this is not done for you, wait at least until everyone is seated before unfolding, and make sure the napkin is on your lap just as the hors d'oeuvres arrive. Large dinner napkins should be left folded in half, so there is a double thickness on your lap, and smaller lunch napkins completely unfolded. The napkin should be left on your lap throughout the meal, except when you need to wipe your mouth. If, during a formal dinner, your napkin slithers off your lap, do not attempt to dive down to rescue it from among other diners' feet. Attract the attention of a waiter who will retrieve the napkin or bring you a fresh one to use.

When it is time to leave, put your napkin on the table. In Europe, it is usual to put the napkin crumpled on to the table to indicate it is ready for laundry. In America, according to Letitia Baldridge, social secretary to the late president, John F. Kennedy, it is more correct to leave it neatly folded on the table when you leave.

Opposite A napkin is left draped over the champagne bucket, ready to be wrapped around the neck of the bottle to catch drips when it is poured. **Below left** A white dinner napkin over the waiter's arm looks smart while protecting his clothes against spills. **Below middle** A napkin wrapped around the neck of a bottle adds a sophisticated note. **Below right** Napkins are sometimes used to hand perfectly polished glasses to guests.

napkins for occasions

From ritzy cocktail parties to friendly suppers, and from formal weddings to picnics on the beach – wherever there is food or drink, napkins are needed. Here you will find ideas to match the napkin to the event, so that functionality is equalled by style and visual effect.

wedding romance

Memorable and romantic, wedding tables have a lot to live up to. The bride needs to adore them because it is, after all, her day. Yet they need to appeal to all generations. White napery is the safest route to follow, but this need not limit you to a traditional look. White can look equally good in a sleek minimalist setting with flowers and napkin ties providing accent colours.

Opposite Candelabras, champagne, and deliciously scented roses; wedding tables don't come any more romantic than this. The deep pink of the roses picks out the floral tones of the best family china, while rose petals, the universal icon of romance, are decoratively scattered along the length of the table to bring colour to the pure white linen.

Below left Classic white napkins are given the romantic treatment with a single red rose, tied in position with a huge lilac organza bow.

Below middle An elegant alternative is to fold the napkin neatly, tie it with narrow ribbon, then tuck in a tiny sprig of a fragrant herb. Choose a woody stemmed variety such as rosemary or lavender, as neither wilt too readily during the course of a meal.

Below right Delightfully feminine and undeniably bridal, this rolled napkin has been tied with a generous length of organza ribbon. Hedgerow flowers, tucked between the folds, evoke sweet-smelling summer meadows.

celebrate in style

Significant events such as anniversaries or naming ceremonies deserve a degree of formality that lends importance to the occasion. A good starting point is to work out a colour scheme that complements the event or the room, and creates a sense of harmony. Use napkins and china that suit the occasion, to pick up the tones of the furniture and décor. Accentuate this further with a clever choice of flowers.

Top The pretty pink floral theme of this table setting is perfectly offset by classic monogrammed linen napkins.
Opposite Deep purple anemones and antique blue plates emphasize the lilac of the chair covers. With such an elegant setting the napkins need only to be very simply folded.
Left A delicate, pink hydrangea floret adds a charming finishing touch to each table setting.

family lunch

Delicious food, simply prepared and set out on a table laid with colourful linen and earthenware crockery, sets the ambience for a warm, friendly family get together, whether inside or out. Keep the mood informal for a relaxed atmosphere. If you are hosting a buffet, plenty of napkins are a good idea; you can use them to mop up spills and to wipe children's sticky hands and faces.

Far left Coloured details add interest and contribute to the informality of a relaxed luncheon table.

Left Take inspiration from the Mediterranean where they know about family entertaining. Keep the look relaxed and informal by using simple napery and pottery. Spread a colourful country-style cloth, then pick out the colours with toning napkins.

Below Filled baguettes wrapped in cheerfully checked napkins look fun when they are assembled en masse. When each napkin is different, there is no arguing whose baguette is whose – particularly important when the younger members of the family prefer to nibble a little, then come back later for more.

Top left Even if the styles are different, with some antique and some modern, white napkins always look good together.

Centre left When entertaining lots of friends, napkins can be mixed and matched. Blue and white always make a fresh combination.

Bottom left A buffet table with plates and napkins piled high, delicious food made from fresh ingredients, plus decorative details such as candles, creates a warm welcoming ambience for a relaxed evening with friends.

Main picture Even the simplest supper setting takes on a seasonal look with the addition of a flower from the garden.

Opposite Napkins wrapped around serving dishes can be used to match the setting of the day, while protecting your hands from the heat.

supper party

Entertaining nowadays is easy, informal and relaxed. Simple dishes using delicious fresh ingredients can be quickly put together and laid out on platters for a visual delight. Avoid making the table setting too fussy; if you do not own enough matching plates or napkins to cater for all your guests, simply mix them then pile them high for an abundant look. The key is to keep to a colour theme: all white, perhaps, so you can mix old and new; shades which are tonally compatible or, on the more adventurous side, those which contrast. If you need to co-ordinate differently coloured china, create harmony within the scheme by choosing a linking shade in the fabric of the napkins.

the cocktail hour

For ritzy cocktail parties to run really smoothly, you need to pay special attention to the practicalities. With everyone standing around, glass in hand, there are bound to be inelegant spills, so equip guests and servers with suitable napkins.

Left Delicately embroidered napkins tucked into champagne glasses give guests a handy wipe to catch drips as drinks are being dispensed or to dab lips or fingertips when the trays of hors d'oeuvres are served.
Above Guests can use napkins to hold their glasses as drinks are being poured, and so catch any spills or droplets.
Opposite The fuss-free simplicity of these pure-white linen napkins looks ultra chic with the geometric lines of classic vermouth glasses.

a summer picnic

Spend memorable summer days with friends and family by packing picnics to take to glorious secluded corners of the countryside, or simply in to the garden. Dainty, floral-patterned cotton table linen evokes summer meadows and will happily mix and match with striped cloths in similar tones.

Opposite Load the car with a fold-up table and brightly striped cloths, teamed with prettily sprigged napkins for a perfect summer picnic. An enamelled jug filled with summer flowers transforms a simple picnic table into a special occasion setting.
Below left Line baskets and wrap china in charming floral napkins that co-ordinate with the rest of the linens. As well as being an attractive way to protect the china while transporting it to the picnic spot, the lined baskets can double up as a delightful way to serve bread, rolls and fruit once the tableware has been taken out.
Right Florals happily mix as long as you choose china and fabrics in a similar tone, with patterns of a similar scale.
Below right Old-fashioned floral napkins give the picnic a traditional English feel.

beach party

Long, lazy lunches by the beach are so much more pleasurable when set up on a trestle table laid with simple napkins and unbreakable enamelware. Choose seaside shades of blues and aquas teamed with plenty of white to keep the look fresh, and go prepared to cope with the elements. Linens need to be anchored down on breezy beaches, so scour the shore for attractive pebbles to keep each napkin decoratively in its place.

Opposite Use pebbles and feathers found on the beach as table decorations, and keep your picnicware simple to reflect that beachcomber's look.

Left Blue and white always make a successful combination at the seaside.

Below Make simple beach-style settings by either wiring, or simply placing, shells on the corners of napkins.

decorated napkins

Exquisite edging, delicate embroidery or a simple motif painted on to one corner transforms a simple square of fabric into a delightful napkin that is all the more gorgeous for the handcrafted detail. The joy is that napkins are small enough for an embroidery detail to be completed with gratifying speed.

Above left White lingerie trimmings can come out of the closet to adorn white napkins.

Above Natural linen and natural raffia make a great modern partnership. Just thread-up the raffia on a darning needle and make generous running stitches.

Above right A border of self-coloured straight stitches is all this shell-pink napkin needs to finish it off.

Left The narrowest velvet ribbon border adds a rich touch to a linen napkin.

Right A trio of silvery beads teamed with simple, modern stainless-steel cutlery, perfectly sets off this coffee-coloured napkin.

Below left A border of toile du jouy stitched on to similar linen, gives a subtle edging.

Below middle White cutwork still looks as fresh as it did in its Victorian heyday. The addition of a glass bead gives this napkin sparkle.

Below right Fresh or silk snowdrops tucked into narrow green satin ribbon lend a delicate, decorative charm to the purest white napkins.

Easy edgings and simple decorative effects can transform plain napkins into something very special. Most can be done by hand, and none take too long. You may also find interesting edges and embellishments on napkins that are available in stores; even if you only buy one or two, rather than a set, they will still come in useful.

Above left Pretty shell discs on a ready-made trim are quick to sew on to a toning napkin.
Above middle Fine lilac organdie takes on a feminine feel with a petticoat-like edging.
Above right A narrow crochet trim has charming feminine appeal while avoiding any hint of frilliness.
Left Frayed edges give napkins a soft, feathery touch, and nothing could be simpler to do.

Below left Four lines of blue stitching make a smart trim for simple white cotton napkins.
Below middle There is little that can better a monogram for elegant, restrained decoration. The best are antique, so scour the bric-à-brac and antique stalls.
Below right Mother-of-pearl buttons that have been threaded on to plain household string make a stunningly simple combination.

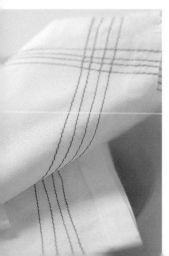

couched organdie

Gossamer light and delicately translucent, organdie has delightful feminine appeal. Naturally stiff, it has surprising body, which means you can not only create light, luminous folds, but it can also be creased to a knife-edged sharpness. Couch a simple motif using cotton string into one corner of each napkin for an embossed effect.

MATERIALS

Ready-made napkin in silk organdie

Tracing paper

Fine felt-tipped pen

Masking tape

Dressmaking pencil

Fine cotton string

Needle

Matching sewing thread

Scissors

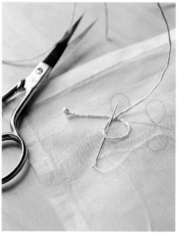

1 Press the napkin flat. Trace the motif from the back of the book using tracing paper and a felt-tipped pen. When the ink has completely dried, tape the motif on to a flat working surface, place the hemmed napkin over the top, positioning the corner over the motif. Tape the napkin in position to fix both the tracing paper and the fabric firmly. Using a dressmaking pencil, carefully trace the motif on to the corner of the napkin. Remove the masking tape securing the napkin.

2 Knot the end of a piece of cotton string and lay the string along the traced design on the corner of the napkin. Using the needle and thread, neatly couch the string in position. When you near the end of the motif, make a knot at this end of the string, trim and stitch down neatly. Iron the couched motif string-side down on a towel, to avoid flattening the string.

decorative edging

The most basic of napkins can take on a new personality with decorative edging. Use restrained ribbon or braid for an elegant city look, or more flamboyant rick-rack for a fresh country feel. If you are deft with a needle, edge napkins with simple embroidery in bold toning or contrasting colours.

ribbon and rick-rack trim

Grosgrain ribbon teamed with rick-rack gives napkins a smart yet pretty edging that is easy to do even if you are not confident at sewing. Use this technique for stitching on any ribbon or braid to give old napkins a new lease of life, or to transform remnants into elegant table linens. This edging of matching grosgrain ribbon and contrasting rick-rack braid makes a neat, yet lively trim for napkins.

1 Cut a square of fabric for each napkin. Turn under a double hem of 1cm/½in around all edges. Pin, tack (baste) and machine stitch all around. To add the ribbon border, cut four lengths of grosgrain ribbon, each 50cm/20in long. Pin one piece along one edge, turning under the ends. Repeat with the opposite side. Pin, tack, then machine stitch all around. Repeat with the remaining two sides.

2 Pin and tack the rick-rack so it overlaps the edge of the ribbon where it meets the napkin. At the corners, simply bend the rick-rack back on itself. Sew in place, turning the ends under where they meet.

MATERIALS

50 x 50cm/20 x 20in of fabric per napkin

Needle and pins

Matching sewing thread

2m/2¼yd grosgrain ribbon 2.5cm/1in wide, per napkin

2m/2¼yd rick-rack trim per napkin

easy embroidery

Simple embroidery can make effective edging, especially if you choose strong colours and make the stitches large for a bold statement. Blanket stitch, oversized oversewing and cross stitch are all easy to do; the knack is to keep them evenly spaced. The traditional way to do this is to count the threads between each stitch, which is not difficult if you are working with a coarse-weave fabric. If you are using a fine-weave fabric, you can make up a card with measured-out marks to use as a guide or use a unit measurement, such as the width of a finger, between each stitch.

Right Lilac blanket stitch on a turquoise napkin gives a lovely folksy feel.
Below left Emerald-green oversized oversewing turns fresh lime napkins into smart linens for a city table.
Below right Cross stitch worked in magenta thread on orange napkins creates a strong contemporary statement.

simple stitching

Used cleverly, embroidery stitches can look highly effective. Depending on the materials you choose, and the size of the stitches you use, highly individual looks and moods can be produced. Running stitch, French knots and daisy stitch have all been employed here to create a French provincial style.

MATERIALS

60 x 60cm/24 x 24in of chambray per napkin

Dressmaking shears

Tape measure

Needle and pins

Blue stranded cotton thread (floss)

Matching sewing thread

Embroidery needle

Red stranded cotton thread (floss)

Embroidery scissors

1 Cut a square of chambray for each napkin. Turn under 1cm/½in around all edges and press. Then turn under a 4cm/1½in hem, mitring the corners as you go (see Stitch Directory). Hand sew the hems using slip stich, or machine stitch all around. Press. Using six strands of blue stranded cotton thread (floss), embroider large running stitches 2.5cm/1in from the edge all around the napkin. Embroider another row of running stitches around the napkin, 5mm/¼in away from the outside edge.

2 Mark out where the daisies, and French knots are to go. Here, a French knot was positioned in each corner, and another every 10cm/4in apart, centred between the lines. A daisy stitch was positioned inbetween the French knots all the way round. Using six strands of red thread (floss), make the French knots (see Stitch Directory). Using six strands of blue thread, make the daisy stitches. When finished, press the napkin right-side down on a towel.

drawn threadwork

For classic elegance, there is no better decoration for napkins than drawn threadwork. It is often used to stunning effect on banqueting linens, yet it is not difficult to do. It is best to choose an even weave fabric that is made from strong fibres, otherwise they will keep snapping as you try to pull them out. Linen is ideal.

MATERIALS

60 x 60cm/24 x 24in linen per napkin

Dressmaking shears

Needle and pins

Tape measure

Contrasting thread

Matching sewing thread

1 Cut a square of linen. Using pins, mark out lines 6cm/2½in in from each edge. Since the hem will be turned back to the drawn threadwork, this will give a finished border of 3cm/1¼in. Make a line of tacking (basting) stitches in contrasting thread in place of the pins.

2 Carefully pull out one of the strands right the way across the fabric. Repeat this on all sides with the required number of threads to give the area you like on both the warp and the weft, so that eventually a square of drawn threads has formed.

3 Press in a small hem all around the raw edges, then fold this edge back to the line of drawn threads to make a double thickness border. Press and tack the hem in place, then mitre the corners (see Stitch Directory). Working with the wrong side towards you, make a line of hem stitches in matching thread, catching three threads at a time and taking in the hem as you go. Repeat this along the top edge of the drawn threads and the lower edge, making the stitches line up to create the holed effect.

hand-painted motif

If stitchery is not your skill, you can use paint to decorate plain napkins. There is an ever-growing choice of suitable fabric paints and pens, specially designed so that the finished work can be pressed with a hot iron to fix the colour. Choose paints for bold all-over designs, thick pens for strong lines and fine pens for details, and bring the outdoors inside with bees, butterflies, ladybirds or even dragonflies.

MATERIALS

Tracing paper

Black felt-tipped pen

Dressmaker's carbon

Set of bought or made-up white napkins

Fabric pens, black and yellow

1 Trace the bee design (see Templates) using tracing paper and a black felt-tipped pen. Position the dressmaker's carbon over the corner of the napkin with the traced design over the top. Draw over the design to transfer it to the fabric.

2 Once traced, mark the outline with a black fabric-dye pen, then fill in with a yellow fabric-dye pen. When dry, iron to fix.

holding
and folding

Mints, dragées, petits fours or other dinner treats can be enfolded in napkins; hot dishes can be carried to the table wrapped in them; bread baskets lined with them. Napkins are far more versatile than simple protection, and can be used at the table in many different ways.

Above left Use two toning napkins knotted together for a simple sculptural effect.

Above Loosely tuck napkins into wine glasses to lend a little height to the table setting.

Above right The simplest folds can be the most effective. Linen napkins, such as these, fall so beautifully there is no need to fuss with them.

Left Fascinate your friends by wrapping up each table setting in an organdie napkin, then tying on a generous satin-edged bow.

Right An Indian glass-bead fastening catches the light, lending sparkle to a simple mustard-coloured napkin.

Below left Apple green after-dinner mints or dragées, tumbling from burgundy napkins, make a charming surprise for each guest.

Below middle Create an element of surprise by tucking napkins into delightful tracing paper pockets.

Below right Parcel up a linen napkin with string and curtain weights to lend an unusual and distinctly Oriental feel to the table.

Knotted, scrunched, tied, or simply doubled over, napkins take on quite different personalities depending on how they are folded. They can also be used for lining baskets and bowls, holding delicate posies of flowers that will reflect any floral displays on the table, or can become the wrapping for a surprise gift for each of your guests.

Above left Enfold pre-starter nibbles in pure white napkins on each side plate.
Above middle Nestle a few flowers into napkins on the table for seasonal appeal.
Above right Napkins used to line bowls add colour and softness to the setting.
Left Sprigs of fresh herbs wrapped in the napkins impart a delicious fragrance that really excites the taste buds.

Below left Sugar mice wrapped in squares of felt in contrasting colours are perfect for a children's party table.
Below middle Tie a napkin around a hot drink in a glass. As well as giving it appeal, it is so much more comfortable to hold.
Below right If you have no time for fancy folding, just loosely knot the napkins, for plates with panache.

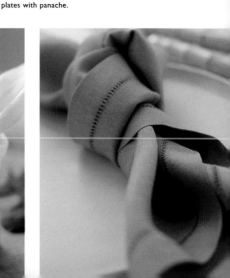

envelope fold

Eminently elegant, this envelope fold can be made in a trice, and is ideal for hosts in a hurry who want to make an impression. It looks smartest in pure linen which falls naturally into soft folds.

1 Fold the napkin in half to form a large rectangle. Next, form a point at one end of the rectangle by folding down each corner towards the centre. This makes the flap of the envelope.

2 Fold the other half of the rectangle over to cover the pointed half. Fold down the corners of the top layer to form another point over the top of the first one.

3 Next, fold the top layer down so the point is just below the folded edge. Crease the fold with your thumb. Fold the second pointed flap over the first so it lies slightly higher than the first and the two pointed flaps are visible.

cutlery roll

Smart braid and clever folding transform a plain napkin into a neat cutlery roll. Cleverly accommodating a four-piece place setting plus a napkin, a roll can be filled up for each guest before setting out for trouble-free picnicking.

MATERIALS

I large napkin per cutlery roll

52cm/21in of braid
4cm/1½in wide for binding

Scissors

Needle and pins

Matching sewing thread

1.7m/5½ft of matching braid
2cm/¾in wide for top edge,
sides, and ties

Contrasting thread

1 Cut a piece of the wider braid the same length as one side of the napkin. Lay it along one edge of the napkin. Pin and tack (baste), then machine stitch along both edges of the braid. Lay the napkin face down on a surface. Fold up the braid-finished edge to a depth that will hold the knife, fork and spoon. Cut two lengths of narrow braid to fit along the top edge. Pin one length to the front of the top edge and one to the back. Stitch through all three layers. Repeat with both side seams, tacking through all the layers. Lay the cutlery over the top of the folded edge and with pins, mark the position of the stitching lines.

3 To make the ties, fold the remaining piece of narrow braid in half and stitch in position halfway down one side between the two napkin layers. Turn in narrow double hems at the ends of the ties, and stitch with matching thread.

2 When you are happy with the spacing, tack the pocket seams and remove the pins. Machine stitch the seams, firmly securing each one at the top using the reverse stitch facility. Remove the tacking threads.

parcelled surprise

On celebration days, such as Christmas, Easter or even at weddings, turn table linen into giftwrapping and give guests a surprise when they unfold their napkins. As well as adding a thoughtful touch to the whole occasion, napkin parcels are an easy way to lend height to the layout of the table.

MATERIALS
For each setting:
I napkin
I gift box containing gift

I Lay a large napkin flat on the table and position the box diagonally on the napkin. Lift two opposite points of the napkin and hold them together.

2 Fold the points down and fold them over again so they lie neatly on the top of the box.

3 Fold in the excess napkin on either side of the box and press flat to form a narrow strip.

4 Now pull the two long corners up together and knot over the box to secure.

buttoned wraps

Edge and encircle napkins with beautiful fabric and create real chic by securing with a natural mother-of-pearl button. You need only small pieces of material so buy the very best for exquisite results. Either make them to match or choose different harmonizing colours and invidualize the wraps for each member of the family.

MATERIALS

A 10 x 17cm/ 4 x 6½in
strip of fabric

Tape measure

Needle and pins

Contrasting thread

Dressmaking shears

Matching sewing thread

Mother-of-pearl button,
2cm/¾in in diameter

I Fold the fabric in half with right sides together to form a strip measuring 5 x 17cm/2 x 6½in. With right sides together, pin, tack (baste) and stitch a 5mm/¼in seam down the long edge. Fold the strip in half lengthwise to find the centre of a short edge, and place a pin at this point. Measure 3cm/1¼in from the top down each side of the strip, and place a pin on each side of the strip. Use these pins as markers to cut a point, which should then be squared off. Pin, tack and stitch the pointed edges together.

2 Turn right-side out. Turn under a 5mm/¼in seam on the straight end of the strip and slip-stitch together. Press. Machine stitch a fine line around the whole napkin ring. Stitch on a mother-of-pearl button at the straight end, and use this to mark the position for the buttonhole at the pointed end. Work the buttonhole with your sewing machine.

cards and flowers

Sharp, origami-inspired napkin folds lend sculpture to minimalist tables. The rolled sections make a perfect holder for place cards and sprigs of leaves or flowers to soften the whole effect. Woody stemmed foliage, such as the rosemary used here, is least likely to wilt. For this napkin fold, choose a densely woven fabric, and starch it well before you begin, so that it will keep its shape.

MATERIALS

I napkin, at least 50cm/20in square

Pins

I place card

Flowers and/or herbs

I Fold the napkin into three to make a narrow rectangular strip. Now mark the centre point of the bottom of the strip and fold up the left side of the napkin at this point.

2 Fold up the right side of the napkin. Turn the napkin over so the point is now at the top. Tightly roll up the lower flaps until they meet the fold. Hold in place with pins.

3 Turn the napkin over so the point is at the bottom. Fold the left-hand side in towards the bottom point, lining up the roll with the central fold. Repeat with the right-hand side so the two rolls face each other and the base is now a square. Add the place card and flowers.

organza sachets

Tuck pastel napkins into delightful translucent organza sachets for a fresh and pretty table setting. The hues will show through, giving a hint of colour, and making an enchanting tinted white-on-white scheme. Decorate each one with a button or tiny seasonal flower, though try to choose varieties that will not wilt too readily.

MATERIALS

58 x 15cm/23 x 6in silk organza per sachet

Needle and pins

Matching sewing thread

Scissors

Buttons or fresh flower-heads

1 On one short side of the silk organza, turn under a double hem of 5mm/¼in, then pin, tack (baste) and stitch. Now measure 24cm/9½in down the length of the fabric from the hemmed end and, with right sides facing out, fold the fabric up at this point to form the bottom of the sachet. Taking a 5mm/¼in seam, pin, tack, then stitch the sides. Trim the edges close to the stitching.

2 Turn the sachet inside out and topstitch to enclose the seams. To make the flap, turn under a 5mm/¼in hem on the right side of the top edge of the sachet, then turn the top section back on itself. Pin, tack and stitch the side edges.

3 Trim close to the edge and turn right-side out and finish the flap hem with a line of machine stitching. Press to finish. Decorate with buttons or flowers at the last minute.

celebrate with paper

Cost effective, cheerful and offering an infinite variety of colours and finishes, paper napkin rings add fun to any party. Browse around art stores for special handmade paper, but remember that more prosaic papers, such as brown wrapping paper, corrugated cardboard, and even newspaper will achieve original effects.

concertina ring

For a fun zigzag napkin ring (far left), crease a sheet of paper into approximately 2.5cm/1in widths along its length and tear off strips. This gives a slightly rough edge, which looks much more interesting than cut edges. Concertina the paper into approximately 2.5cm/1in creases and punch holes through all the layers. Test the ring for length around a napkin. Now thread coloured paper ribbon through the holes and tie.

layered paper ring

Create any colour scheme you like by layering paper shade on shade to make this napkin ring (left). Start by tearing a 2.5cm/1in wide strip of paper into 17cm/6¼in lengths. Tear a slightly shorter and narrower length of contrasting paper and fix this on top using paper glue. Finally, add a torn paper square in the centre. Once the napkin ring is dry, punch a hole in each end, thread string through and tie to secure.

paper bow

A large paper bow (above) adds fun to a basic paper napkin ring. Simply tear a strip of blue paper, bring the ends to the middle, wrap a strip of lime paper around the centre and glue to fix. Finally, glue the whole bow to the ring.

paper fan

Fans (above) lend a touch of frivolity to party time. Simply concertina a small piece of paper, fold in half and glue the centre together to form the fan, then glue the whole ensemble on to a basic paper napkin ring.

napkin pocket

Transform simple napkins into exquisite pockets for storing linens in scented cupboards or drawers. A plain piqué cotton napkin can be made to look very special with clever folding and the addition of an imaginative fastener. With the hems already finished off, there is little fiddly sewing to be done.

MATERIALS

White piqué napkin, approximately 45cm/18in square

Matching sewing thread

Needle

Ready-made rolled fastener

1 Fold the napkin in half and then in half again, and run your thumb down the folds to make strong creases. Unfold, then fold the corners to the centre so they meet where the original creases cross. Make sure all the edges butt together and then press.

2 Slip stitch the edges together down two sides of one point, leaving one side open like the flap of an envelope. Make extra stitches where the corners meet, for extra strength.

3 Sew one part of the rolled fastener on to the loose flap and mark where it will join the other part of the fastener on the sewn section. Stitch the fastener firmly into position.

frogged fasteners

The elaborate looks of classic Chinese frogging belie their simplicity – all you need is a length of cord and a needle and thread to make these most decorative of fasteners. Once you have mastered this simple one, you can experiment to make ever-more intricate versions.

MATERIALS

2 x 50cm/20in lengths of

cord, 5mm/⅕in thick

Needle and pins

Matching sewing thread

1 Make a Turk's head knot (or similar) a third of the way along one of the lengths of cord, following the diagrams in the Stitch Directory.

2 This is a complicated knot to accomplish and may take you a few attempts, but once you have completed one the others will be easier.

3 Take one end of the cord and roll it inwards towards the knot. Stitch the roll firmly in place as you go. Do the same with the other end, remembering to catch with stitches as you work. When half the cord is used up (about 15cm/6in), fold the remainder in half and roll from the fold inwards so you end up with a knot and three rolls. Stitch the rolls together.

4 Fold the other length of cord in thirds and mark these with a pin. Starting at one end, roll the cord inwards towards the first marker, stitching as you go. Once you are about 5mm/¼in from the pin, stitch to finish off. Roll up the other length to form two circles in the same way as the other portion of the fastener. When you get 5mm/¼in from the centre, stitch to finish off. Stitch the rolls together, leaving a top loop for fastening to the knot.

antique-effect finery

Scour department stores or bric-à-brac stalls for napkins that are exquisitely embroidered, have interesting edgings, intricate cutwork or drawn threadwork, then give them a fold and several stitches to make beautiful pockets with all the detail of antique originals. Add a beautiful mother-of-pearl or bone button, and nobody will believe you made them yourself.

Above A cutwork napkin is turned into a pocket with simple side seams made by stitching the wrong sides together to allow the scalloping to become a feature. The flap is held down on each side by a wooden button tied on with string.

Left A prettily embroidered and scallop-edged napkin is quickly turned into a charming pocket once the corners are folded in and scalloped edges caught in place. A delightful flower-shaped button provides the finishing touch.

Opposite Here, a smart antique French napkin has been folded over to form a pocket and fastened by cord wound around two buttons.

napkin book

Napkins tucked into the string inside this special linen book are kept in their pristine laundered state until they are needed on the table. This one is made from an antique French napkin or dish towel.

MATERIALS

Rough linen napkin or dish towel

Tape measure

Fine brown household string

Scissors

Masking tape

Matching sewing thread

Needle

Napkins for inside the holder

1 Fold the napkin or towel into three to make a long, thin rectangle. Measure the napkin, double the measurement and add on 10–12cm/4–4½in. Cut three strands of string to this length and knot them at one end. Tape to a surface and make a long plait (braid).

2 Keep the holder folded, then fold it inwards into thirds. Place the napkins inside, then tie the plait along the crease made by the back third to hold the napkins in place.

3 To form the fastener, plait (braid) another small section of string and attach this to the string at the back of the napkin holder. The knot at the end forms a small button. To make the buttonhole simply make a loop of string and knot. Attach this firmly to the front side of the napkin holder so the stitches do not show. When closed, the holder folds into three and makes a firm and attractive 'book'.

Left Antique linen which has been laundered many times has a wonderful weight and quality that simply cannot be matched by new linen. Search out dish towels like this one on bric-à-brac stalls for making inexpensive yet fine napkin books.

napkin rings

With imagination and creativity, napkins can be dressed with rings or ties that are fashioned from a wide variety of materials, selected to complement the setting and inspire the diner. Attention to detail will make your guests feel that they are welcome, as well as helping to create a special dining environment.

Above left A pipe-cleaner bent into curly shapes makes the most unlikely napkin ring. If you choose your colours carefully, the effect can be stunning.

Above middle Tied tape trimmed with shells is inexpensive, easy to do and a simply delightful way to tidy the napkins.

Above right A diamanté buckle makes a glamorous ring for a finely woven, pale pink napkin.

Left Twisted twigs and beads make the most unlikely materials for napkin rings, but they look stunning against white linen.

Right These hydrangea florets match the delicate willow green of the napkin perfectly, making an ideal decoration for a simple raffia tie.

Below left Glass beads and wire, fashioned into a ring, take on a jewel-like appearance.

Below middle A flamboyant scarlet ribbon, tied in a bow, contrasts beautifully with a luxurious purple napkin.

Below right Piping cord, finger-knitted into a chain, perfectly complements a white-and-blue checked napkin.

Dress up your napkins with rings and ties to lend a sense of occasion to the table setting. The same linens can take on quite a different personality, depending on whether they are clasped with a jewel, trimmed with beads, or tied with a seasonal bloom. Napkin rings can be bought, made, or quickly fashioned from simple lengths of ribbon.

Above left In high summer, a row of silk daisies looks enchanting when tied on to pastel-coloured checked napkins.

Above middle A short length of ribbon with a floret tucked in the knot makes a sweetly simple napkin ring.

Above right Plaited (braided) cords lend a Celtic feel to elegant grey linen napkins.

Left Several strings of threaded beads make excellent napkin rings.

Below left Brightly coloured beaded wire bent into a flower shape, then attached to a ring of spiralling wire, makes for a glorious napkin ring accessory.

Below middle Buttoned-up string in pistachio green looks confident, fresh and very contemporary.

Below right Brightly coloured long glass beads threaded on to wire make a vibrant bracelet-like napkin ring.

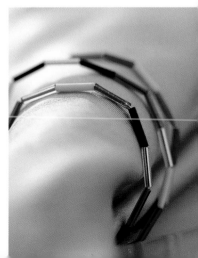

paper table treats

Crisp and smart, there is something rather lovely about the juxtaposition of pure white paper with traditional starched linen. Paper napkin rings may seem throwaway, but with a little imagination and good sharp creases, they can be made very special indeed.

MATERIALS

**A4 (29 x 42cm/11½ x 16½in)
sheets of cartridge paper**

Scissors

Thread or fine wire

Double-sided tape

Paper glue

I Cut a sheet of cartridge paper in half crosswise and firmly fold both pieces into sharp, narrow accordion pleats.

2 Secure the paper in the centre with a piece of thread or wire. Snip diagonally across both ends of the pleats to form points.

3 Fan out the paper to form a star. Turn under the corner of two end points and fold back once to secure the shape. Make a ring of paper joined at the back by double-sided tape, then fix to the back of the star.

paper lantern

To make the lantern (far right), cut a piece of paper about 21 x 15cm/8½ x 6in. Fold it in half lengthwise to measure 7.5cm/3in x 21cm/8½in and make a series of cuts 1cm/½in apart from the folded side of the paper, finishing about 2.5cm/1in before you reach the cut edges. Unfold the paper. Stick the short ends together to complete the lantern.

a touch of gold ...

Gold decoration on pure white china makes a glorious combination and lends an air of celebration to any occasion. Fine coaching lines encase pretty gold dots which are also echoed on the plates. Although simple to achieve, the design creates impact with an elegant overall effect. Use water-based gouache paint, if you prefer to restore the napkin rings to their pure white form after the occasion, or gold ceramic paint for a more permanent, washable result.

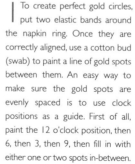

1 To create perfect gold circles, put two elastic bands around the napkin ring. Once they are correctly aligned, use a cotton bud (swab) to paint a line of gold spots between them. An easy way to make sure the gold spots are evenly spaced is to use clock positions as a guide. First of all, paint the 12 o'clock position, then 6, then 3, then 9, then fill in with either one or two spots in-between.

2 Once the spots are dry, touch in the elastic bands with gold using the cotton bud (swab) or a very fine artist's paintbrush.

MATERIALS

2 small white elastic bands per napkin ring

White china napkin ring

Cotton buds (swabs)

Gold gouache or ceramic paint

Artist's paintbrush

... silver service

Silvery stainless steel brings a stylish glint to contemporary table settings. Tie one end of a length of shirring elastic to the ring at the bottom of one of the safety pins. Thread on the rest of the safety pins. When you get to the end, undo the tied end, then tie the two ends together in a reef knot. Shuffle the pins along to hide the knot. Now repeat the same process with a new piece of shirring elastic at the other end of the pins to complete the napkin ring.

filigree beading

These delightful, intricate-looking beaded napkin rings are surprisingly robust. Made from glass embroidery beads and threaded on to silvery galvanized wire, they have a sparkle that is reminiscent of diamanté. Altogether, they provide the perfect accessory for a romantic evening.

MATERIALS

Galvanized wire or beading wire

Scissors or wire cutters

Pliers

Glass embroidery beads

1 Cut a long length of galvanized or beading wire. Use pliers to turn under one end to stop the beads from slipping off. Thread the beads on to the wire, then bend the other end to secure them.

2 Fashion the beaded wire into a flower shape and secure the 'petals' by wrapping the beaded wire around the centre. Make a ring from another piece of wire threaded with beads, and attach the flower head to this with wire.

beaded initial

Once you have mastered the knack of beading, experiment with any shape you like. Initials add a personal touch to each place setting.

snowflake

Wire beading can take on a sculptural feel, but if you don't have the time, look out for store-bought examples, like this snowflake.

fretwork-style felt

Felt doesn't fray, so it can easily be cut into fabulously intricate shapes – and there is no need to hem around fiddly corners. So, equipped with the sharpest scissors you can find, there is no end to the designs you can cut.

1 Cut a 7cm/2¾in strip of felt from one of the squares. Trace the outline of the template at the end of the book and transfer to cardboard or stiff paper and use as a pattern. Cut a second 7cm/2¾in strip of felt in a contrasting colour. Place the pattern on to the strip.

2 Trace around the pattern using a pen, then cut out the shape with embroidery scissors.

3 Using fabric glue, stick the fretwork pattern to the napkin ring or hand-sew it on using small running stitches. Turn under a 1cm/½in hem along each long side of the napkin ring to give it a little stiffness. Stitch a small button to one end and cut a hole at the other end for fastening.

star place cards

Draw a star on paper and transfer this to stiff paper or cardboard. Cut out the star from felt, embroider an initial on it, then glue to a piece of stiff folded cardboard or cartridge paper.

MATERIALS

Different-coloured 21cm/8½in squares of felt

Tape measure

Scissors for paper

Tracing paper and pencil

Stiff paper or cardboard to make a template

Pen

Very sharp embroidery scissors

Fabric glue

Needle and pins

Matching sewing thread

A small button per napkin ring

foil place tags

Avoid awkward moments when seating guests by giving every setting a place name. Luggage style labels, crafted from foil, are practical, pleasing and give a modern twist to classic white table linen. The silver of the tags complements the tableware perfectly. For each place tag, cut two pieces of modelling foil, measuring 4 x 6cm/1½ x 2½in. Stick the two pieces together using double-sided tape to make the label more substantial. Trim off the top corners for a traditional luggage-label shape. Emboss the design or initial using a soft pencil on the wrong side. Punch a hole in the tag and thread the silver ribbon through, then tie around the napkin with ribbon.

fine wirework

It is always thrilling when you can transform the most prosaic of household items into something quite beautiful. If it is quick and easy, so much the better. These simple wire ideas fall right into that category, and make wonderful napkin holders.

hovering bee

This witty and original bee-on-a-wire (left) makes an elegant but minimal napkin ring. To make it, simply turn in one end of a piece of galvanized wire to avoid injury, then wrap the wire around any cylindrical object you like, such as a bottle or a rolling pin, depending on how tight you want the spiral to be; bear in mind that the napkin needs to be able to slip through. Cut the wire using wire cutters, remove the object, and attach a bee, bead, or anything else that appeals, on to the elongated end of the wire.

electric inspiration

Fine filigree work is easily fashioned from black electrical wire (below). First, separate the wire, then cut into manageable lengths. Bend the wire into circles, dragonfly shapes, letters, hearts, or whatever takes your fancy, then trim with beads or crystals.

Below left Plait (braid) three wires and add a silver bead for an elegant, simple ring. **Below middle** A trio of medallions makes a bold contrast with a classic white napkin. **Below right** A simple dragonfly makes a witty detail on a slender wire ring.

napkin themes

Inexpensive, easy to adapt and simple to stitch, napkins can become the major players in themed table settings. Few of us can change our china or cutlery for a one-off occasion, but it is easy to adapt the napkins or invest in an inexpensive new set to give the table a completely new look.

Above left Add the brightly coloured prints of Provençal fabrics to simple earthenware china for a table setting that evokes long sunny days.

Above middle Green crockery – whatever the period or style – matched with white linen, always looks gives a fresh and summery feel to a table setting.

Above right Give an Oriental-style tea party and serve jasmine tea in a squat teapot and tiny bowls, with roughly-textured napkins on the side.

Left Bend a piece of silver wire into a heart shape and entwine with wool for an instant Valentine feel.

Right Napkins with a simple striped pattern create a rustic mood, perfect for picnics or impromptu meals.

Below left For a Japanese style occasion ensure that you use neutral tones and simple shapes.

Below middle Blue and white is a classic combination that will never date and will suit many styles and themes.

Below right Seasonal flowers, such as this summer daisy, immediately offer a colour scheme that looks right for the time of year.

You can create endlessly different themed tablesettings, yet still use the mainstays from your china cupboard. Simply use inexpensive napkins and witty embellishments to give a different look each time. The theme doesn't have to be elaborate, but can just be enough to give your event a certain distinction and style.

Above left Use white napery, silver accessories and filmy ribbon for a christening.
Above middle Mix colours with confidence by picking out the tones of a design.
Above right Clashing colours with touches of gold evoke the Indian subcontinent.
Left Create a traditional mood with delicately patterned plates matched with the palest pink linen and fresh garden roses.

Below left Geometric designs and florals mix together happily if you choose designs that are of a similar scale and colour.
Below middle Choose a chiffon scarf or fabric to tie up a tiny parcel. Add a sprig of greenery for a fresh modern style.
Below right Sea-greens and blues, and a tiny shell stitched on to the corner of the napkin, help to evoke a beach-party feel.

oriental tables

The simplicity and harmony of Oriental table settings provide a welcome antidote to today's increasingly demanding lifestyles: plain plates and folded napkins in neutral or earth colours are positioned with little adornment on bare tables. If this is somewhat stark for your taste, you could choose a white or neutral cloth and add a single flower or stem in a glass or porcelain vase together with a touch of raffia. This elegant, restrained look can turn a quick stir-fry into a special occasion, although you do not have to wait until you are accomplished with a wok before you give it a try.

Above Create a warm, relaxed country style by using bamboo-handled cutlery, rush plates, and bowls in a deep glaze to blend with natural-coloured napkins.
Left Chopsticks, tied with raffia and placed in serried ranks on toning napkins, have an Eastern charm that makes for easy entertaining. But you need not wait until you are able to serve Oriental meals; regular cutlery tied with raffia would look just as good.
Opposite A matt black bowl provides elegant contrast to a rolled-up coarse-weave napkin in natural cream. The beargrass-wrapped stone provides Japanese styling.

white on white

Whatever your style, you can be confident that white will work. Always elegant, it is the darling of top chefs because it complements all types of food perfectly. At home, it will prove a good investment because you can mix, match and add to white over the years. If you only ever buy one set of napkins, pure white linen or double damask has to be the best investment. They may appear to be extravagant at the time, but both launder beautifully, and will retain their quality no matter how much you use them. Choose pure whites for sophistication, perhaps adding exquisitely scented flowers, or creamy whites for warm elegance.

Opposite Smooth-sided blue-white porcelain enhances the style of these elaborately pleated napkins.

Below left Crunchy, woven, off-white, drawn-threadwork cotton napkins look gorgeous tied simply with pure cotton household string.

Below middle Unfussy, modern, creamy-white china is offset by contemporary linens in crisp textural weaves.

Below right Add a sweetly scented gardenia and tiny rhinestones to the simplest of white settings, and suddenly it is undeniably pretty.

splash of green

For an instant change of mood on your table, add a splash of colour. Fashion has come off the catwalk to influence interiors, and if you want to set your table with your current favourite shade, the best idea is to indulge in some new napkins. Many high-street stores stock inexpensive cotton sets in all the latest hues, or, failing that, buy a metre of fabric off the roll and make your own. They will probably be less expensive than a vase of flowers, and create instant impact.

Left As the winter nights draw in, contrast cosy winter colours, like burgundy and purple, with soft greens.
Above Apple-green and fuchsia-pink create a glorious summertime theme.
Opposite Team deep turquoise-blue china with fresh, spring-green plates and linens for a light-hearted springtime look.

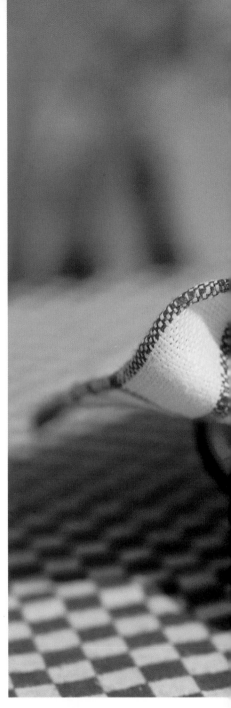

china blues

The fresh combination of china blue and white seems destined never to date. It has managed to top the popularity stakes for more than 200 years since 18th-century Chinese imports inspired Josiah Spode to design the ever popular Willow Pattern. Unlikely to fall from favour now, blue-and-white napkins are a useful linen cupboard mainstay, especially if you choose smart checks and stripes.

Far left Blue-and-white checks and stripes can be mixed endlessly, so they make good bric-à-brac finds. Team classic windowpane weaves with smaller checks, and add both bold and narrow stripes. Do not worry if the blues are not an exact match, but bear in mind that while two different shades could look like a mistake, three or more look planned.

Left Checks in different sizes mix and match beautifully. Pick up the blue of the linens in the decoration of the tableware, as in these tin plates.

Below These denim napkins lend a modern touch to classic blue china.

Opposite A pure white setting is given the festive touch
with a few ivy leaves and sparkling coloured glass.
Above Golden tassels and cord lend an elegant touch of
classic Christmas glamour to antique monogrammed napkins.
Right Gold twine, tied parcel-style, transforms classic white
napkins into a festive visual treat.

festive mood

Buying special Christmas tableware can be an extravagance that proves too costly for
the time of year. Plan, instead, to add festive touches with napkins and accessories
that add the glamour and glitter. This is the time of the year when you can go over
the top with gold and silver to bring sparkle to the festivities.

nature tables

Work with the seasons to keep your table settings fresh. By taking inspiration from nature, the table will always look instinctively right, yet it will often cost absolutely nothing and the raw materials are just outside your door. The key to a successful ambience is to add just the smallest sprig, leaf, berry or flower to capture the natural scene of the season, without gilding the lily.

Opposite Summertime pink or red, in the form of any flower fresh from the garden, makes a glorious summer scheme. Use with napkins of the same colour for a stronger look.
Below left In winter, red-and-white checked napkins look fabulous given a ring of twigs entwined with berries and ivy.

Below centre Add fallen leaves in tones of russet and orange to autumnal-coloured napkins, and conjure up the season of mists and fruitfulness.
Below right Tiny mottled quail's eggs are available at high-street supermarkets. Teamed with a yellow napkin and a primrose flower-head, they make an enchanting springtime detail.

victorian elegance

Delicate floral-printed English bone china still evokes Victorian teatime elegance. The best designs are original bone-china antiques with their dainty shapes and subtle, softened hues, so visit junk stores and bric-à-brac stalls for the prettiest examples. You may not be able to find a matching set, but by teaming pieces with pretty napkins, you will simply add to the charm.

Above This pretty teapot with matching cups makes a perfect breakfast set. Team it with a crisp jacquard-woven linen napkin to protect against spills.

Left Traditional florals team well with contemporary checks, as long as the colours are co-ordinated.

Right Drawn threadwork cotton napkins team beautifully with the more elaborate floral tableware designs.

classical napkin folds

Crisp damask napkins folded into tall sculptural shapes immediately transform even the simplest of table settings into one worthy of the most formal occasions. Most napkin folds are easy to accomplish because they are designed to be made at speed.

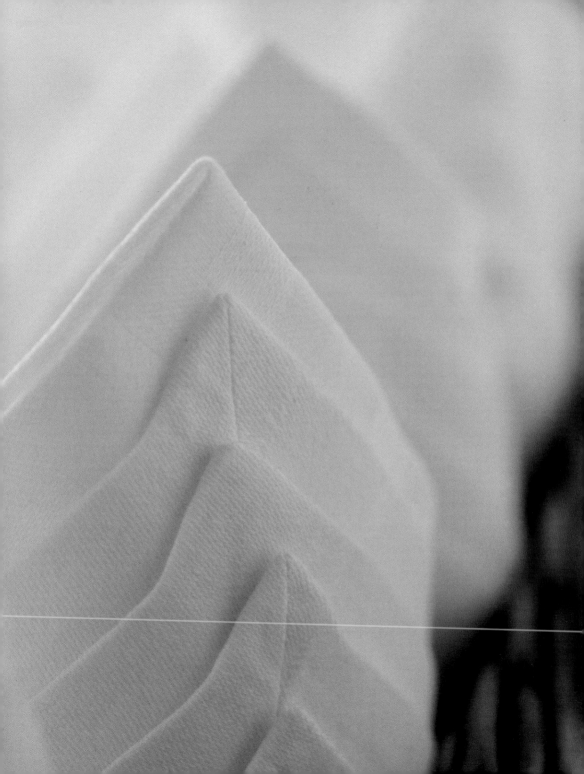

Above left The Cable, an understated fold, is ideal as a contrast on an elaborately decorated table.

Above middle Chevrons, a neat and simple design.

Above right The Clown's Hat is ideal for large numbers.

Left The Cockscomb, an elaborate and impressive design.

Right The Diamon is, a complex and impressive fold.

Below left The Double Swan is ideal for formal occasions.

Below middle The Opera House, a grandly flamboyant and contemporary design.

Below right The Slipper makes a sweetly charming design.

Opposite page: Top left The French Lily, a classic fold with heraldic roots that is perfect for formal dining.

Top middle The Lovers' Knot has a particularly contemporary look when folded in a coloured napkin.

Top right The Flame, a spectacular, sophisticated design.

Right The Mitre is the stately king of napkin folds.

Far right The Carousel, complex but well worth the effort.

Bottom left The Starfish is ideal for a large party.

Bottom middle The Fan, a simple, traditional design.

Bottom right The Wave, a smart design easy to achieve.

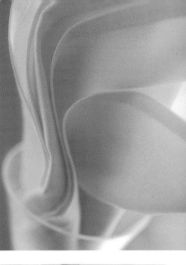

The beautiful symmetry of these classic napkins folds is traditionally shown to best advantage with white napkins. The quality of the linen is shown to its best advantage, and the crisp folds, tucks and peaks are defined by the simplicity of pure white fabric. Use coloured fabrics too, for a much more contemporary look, or to fit in with a theme or occasion.

the wave

Smart yet simple to do, the wave has a tailored look that gives the table an elegant finish. It is an excellent choice when you are entertaining large parties of sit-down guests as it is quick to fold, yet gives a lot more fullness than napkins straight from the cupboard.

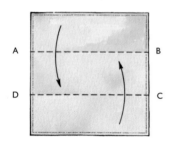

1 Fold the napkin into thirds horizontally.

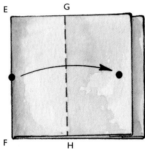

4 Fold dot to dot again, creasing only lightly along GH.

2 Fold in each end.

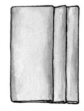

5 The completed wave will look like this.

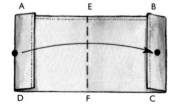

3 Fold dot to dot, as shown, creasing only lightly along EF.

the starfish

When you want to add height to the table, yet you're pushed for time, use the starfish, a chic triangular fold with a good spread base that makes it stand up well. The starfish provides a smart look for long, thin tables.

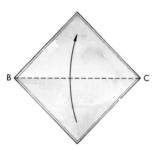

1 Fold the napkin in half diagonally.

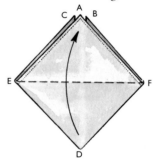

4 Bring the bottom point up to meet the top corners.

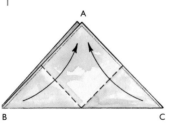

2 Fold corners B and C up to the top of the triangle, as shown.

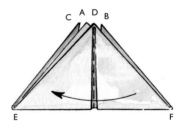

5 Fold the triangle in half to complete.

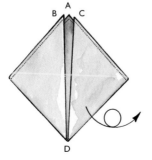

3 The napkin will now look like this. Turn it over.

6 Arrange on its longest side.

the flame

This is a spectacular fold that does justice to any special occasion. In pure white or cream, the flame takes on a sophisticated lily-look, perfect for weddings. An orange or red colour would make a striking choice for lively dinner parties.

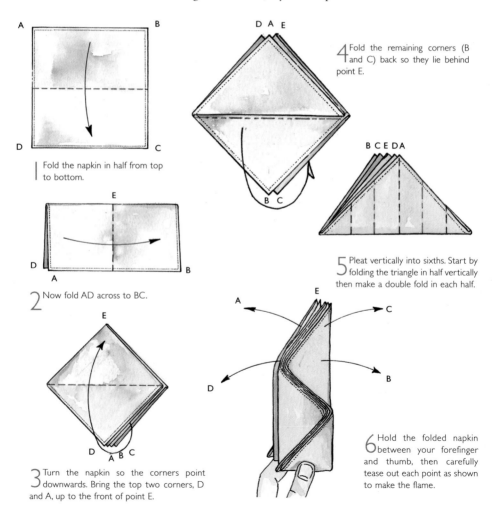

1 Fold the napkin in half from top to bottom.

2 Now fold AD across to BC.

3 Turn the napkin so the corners point downwards. Bring the top two corners, D and A, up to the front of point E.

4 Fold the remaining corners (B and C) back so they lie behind point E.

5 Pleat vertically into sixths. Start by folding the triangle in half vertically then make a double fold in each half.

6 Hold the folded napkin between your forefinger and thumb, then carefully tease out each point as shown to make the flame.

chevrons

For height without the fuss, Chevrons provide a neat solution. Choose napkins made of a good heavy linen, damask or cotton for a generous column-like finished effect.

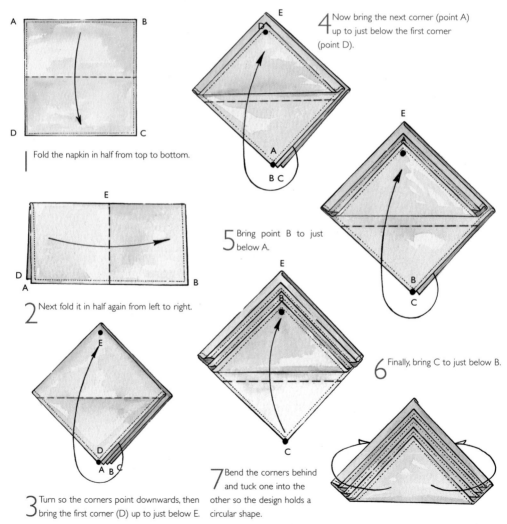

Fold the napkin in half from top to bottom.

2 Next fold it in half again from left to right.

3 Turn so the corners point downwards, then bring the first corner (D) up to just below E.

4 Now bring the next corner (point A) up to just below the first corner (point D).

5 Bring point B to just below A.

6 Finally, bring C to just below B.

7 Bend the corners behind and tuck one into the other so the design holds a circular shape.

the cockscomb

Here is an impressive fold that works best when used for smaller, more intimate occasions. A few cockscombs on a table transform a simple dinner setting into something much more special.

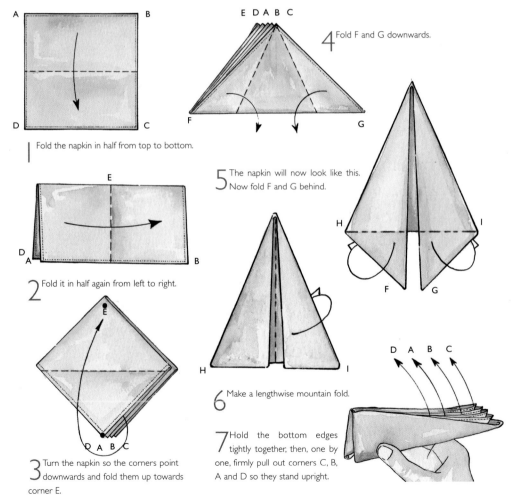

1 Fold the napkin in half from top to bottom.

2 Fold it in half again from left to right.

3 Turn the napkin so the corners point downwards and fold them up towards corner E.

4 Fold F and G downwards.

5 The napkin will now look like this. Now fold F and G behind.

6 Make a lengthwise mountain fold.

7 Hold the bottom edges tightly together, then, one by one, firmly pull out corners C, B, A and D so they stand upright.

the diamond

There is nothing ostentatious about the Diamond; this simple-looking fold is seriously chic and will add flair to the smartest of tables. Mastering the fold, however, could take a little practice!

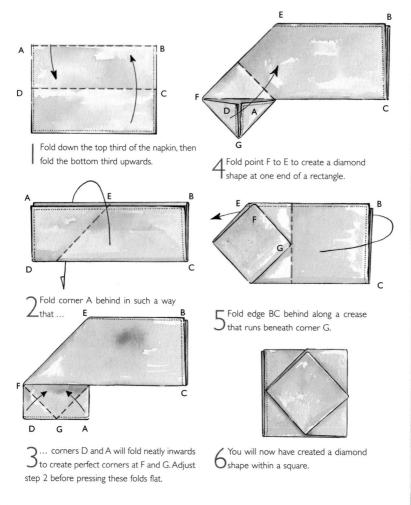

1 Fold down the top third of the napkin, then fold the bottom third upwards.

2 Fold corner A behind in such a way that ...

3 ... corners D and A will fold neatly inwards to create perfect corners at F and G. Adjust step 2 before pressing these folds flat.

4 Fold point F to E to create a diamond shape at one end of a rectangle.

5 Fold edge BC behind along a crease that runs beneath corner G.

6 You will now have created a diamond shape within a square.

the french lily

A charming traditional fold, the French Lily is reminiscent of the fleur-de-lys, so popular in heraldry with all its classical connotations. Choose large, well-starched napkins for this one, as it will help to hold the lily in shape.

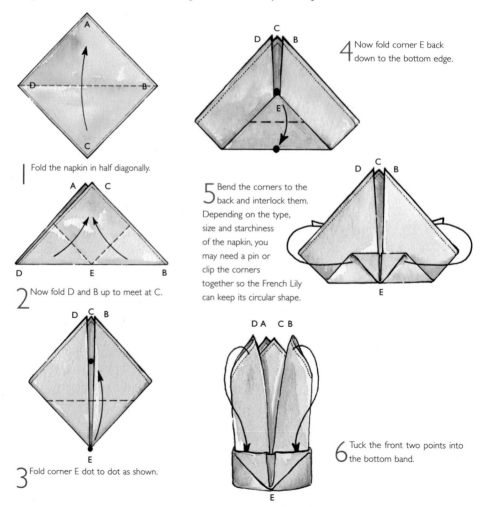

1 Fold the napkin in half diagonally.

2 Now fold D and B up to meet at C.

3 Fold corner E dot to dot as shown.

4 Now fold corner E back down to the bottom edge.

5 Bend the corners to the back and interlock them. Depending on the type, size and starchiness of the napkin, you may need a pin or clip the corners together so the French Lily can keep its circular shape.

6 Tuck the front two points into the bottom band.

the clown's hat

Tall and smart, clowns' hats look wonderful standing on plates along the length of a long dinner table. Their simple shape makes an unfussy silhouette that works well in quantity. Using two different tones of napkins gives a light and shade effect to these distinctive shapes.

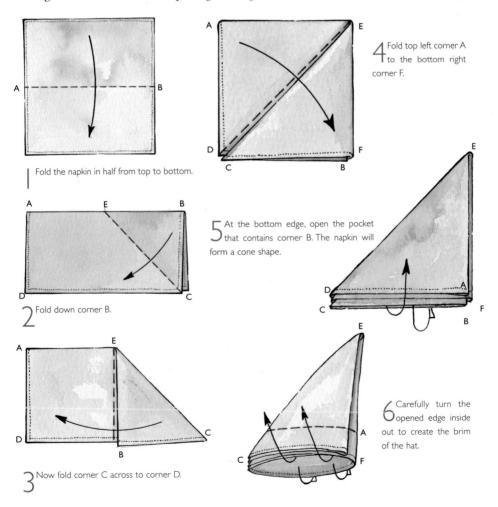

1 Fold the napkin in half from top to bottom.

2 Fold down corner B.

3 Now fold corner C across to corner D.

4 Fold top left corner A to the bottom right corner F.

5 At the bottom edge, open the pocket that contains corner B. The napkin will form a cone shape.

6 Carefully turn the opened edge inside out to create the brim of the hat.

the lovers' knot

A neat twist on every plate looks elegant and modern in a contemporary setting. A lovers' knot is a tidy way to keep larger napkins under control, and looks good in even the brightest of colours.

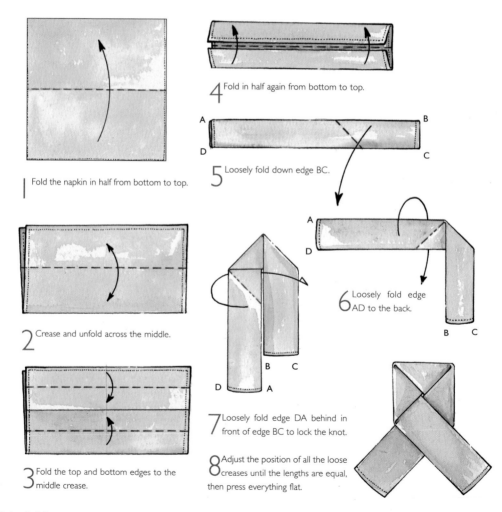

1 Fold the napkin in half from bottom to top.

2 Crease and unfold across the middle.

3 Fold the top and bottom edges to the middle crease.

4 Fold in half again from bottom to top.

5 Loosely fold down edge BC.

6 Loosely fold edge AD to the back.

7 Loosely fold edge DA behind in front of edge BC to lock the knot.

8 Adjust the position of all the loose creases until the lengths are equal, then press everything flat.

the mitre

This fold is a classic that has almost become the symbol of napkin folding. Smart and majestic, this is best reserved for the most formal of occasions. Despite its grandness, the mitre is very quick and easy to do.

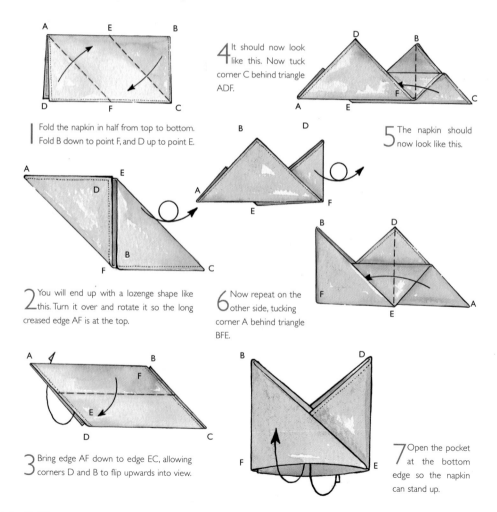

1 Fold the napkin in half from top to bottom. Fold B down to point F, and D up to point E.

2 You will end up with a lozenge shape like this. Turn it over and rotate it so the long creased edge AF is at the top.

3 Bring edge AF down to edge EC, allowing corners D and B to flip upwards into view.

4 It should now look like this. Now tuck corner C behind triangle ADF.

5 The napkin should now look like this.

6 Now repeat on the other side, tucking corner A behind triangle BFE.

7 Open the pocket at the bottom edge so the napkin can stand up.

the double swan

The stately Double Swan makes an elegant statement on the smartest of tables. For all its sophistication, it is not difficult to do, so it is a viable option for large formal occasions. Stunning in white double damask, this fold also looks good in pastel shades.

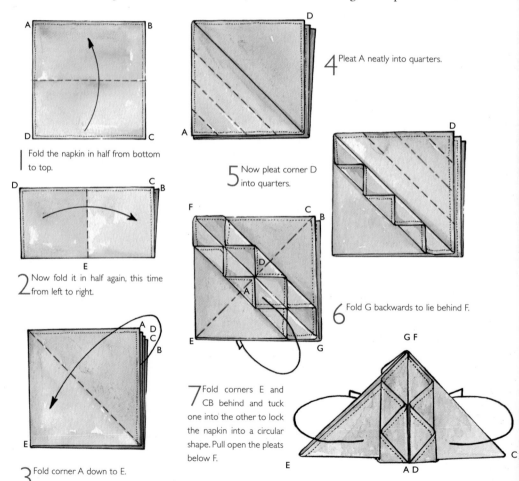

1 Fold the napkin in half from bottom to top.

2 Now fold it in half again, this time from left to right.

3 Fold corner A down to E.

4 Pleat A neatly into quarters.

5 Now pleat corner D into quarters.

6 Fold G backwards to lie behind F.

7 Fold corners E and CB behind and tuck one into the other to lock the napkin into a circular shape. Pull open the pleats below F.

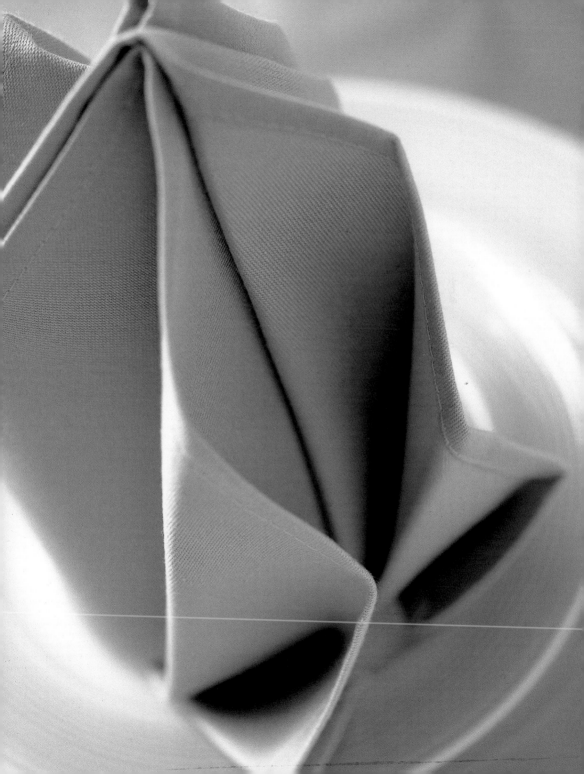

the cable

Neat and unassuming, the cable has a hidden surprise. Its integral pocket can be used to tuck in cutlery – a bonus if serving a buffet as each "roll" can be prepared and stacked at one end of the table.

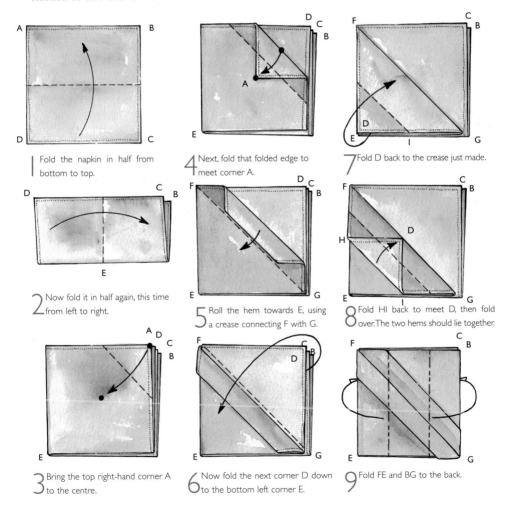

1 Fold the napkin in half from bottom to top.

4 Next, fold that folded edge to meet corner A.

7 Fold D back to the crease just made.

2 Now fold it in half again, this time from left to right.

5 Roll the hem towards E, using a crease connecting F with G.

8 Fold HI back to meet D, then fold over. The two hems should lie together.

3 Bring the top right-hand corner A to the centre.

6 Now fold the next corner D down to the bottom left corner E.

9 Fold FE and BG to the back.

the slipper

Winsome fairytale slippers lend a magical touch to celebration tables. Each napkin makes one slipper; a pair on each plate makes the setting even more appealing. A tiny stick-on gem adds a witty touch to this charming napkin fold.

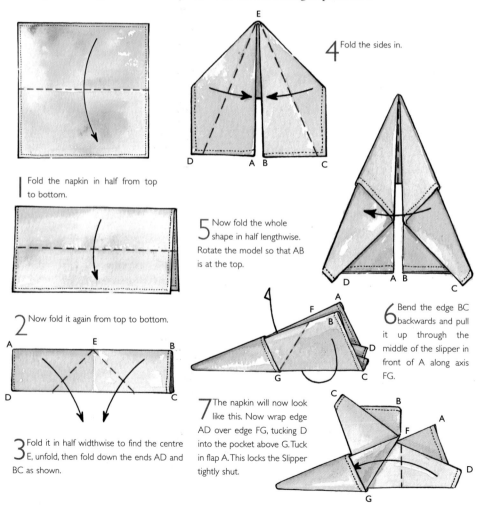

1 Fold the napkin in half from top to bottom.

2 Now fold it again from top to bottom.

3 Fold it in half widthwise to find the centre E, unfold, then fold down the ends AD and BC as shown.

4 Fold the sides in.

5 Now fold the whole shape in half lengthwise. Rotate the model so that AB is at the top.

6 Bend the edge BC backwards and pull it up through the middle of the slipper in front of A along axis FG.

7 The napkin will now look like this. Now wrap edge AD over edge FG, tucking D into the pocket above G. Tuck in flap A. This locks the Slipper tightly shut.

the opera house

Reminiscent of Sydney Harbour's landmark opera house, this is a modern interpretation of the classic tall folds such as the mitre and the French lily, and is best made with a large, well-starched napkin.

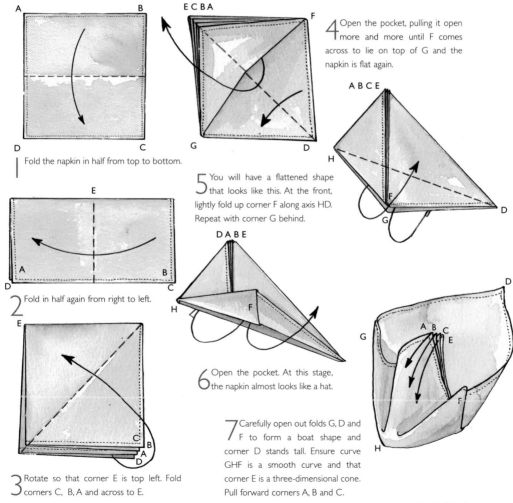

1 Fold the napkin in half from top to bottom.

2 Fold in half again from right to left.

3 Rotate so that corner E is top left. Fold corners C, B, A and across to E.

4 Open the pocket, pulling it open more and more until F comes across to lie on top of G and the napkin is flat again.

5 You will have a flattened shape that looks like this. At the front, lightly fold up corner F along axis HD. Repeat with corner G behind.

6 Open the pocket. At this stage, the napkin almost looks like a hat.

7 Carefully open out folds G, D and F to form a boat shape and corner D stands tall. Ensure curve GHF is a smooth curve and that corner E is a three-dimensional cone. Pull forward corners A, B and C.

the carousel

For height with a modern feel, the carousel is the perfect answer. One of the few napkin folds with a full circular feel, it fills the side plate with pleasing symmetry. Perfecting the carousel, however, takes a little practice.

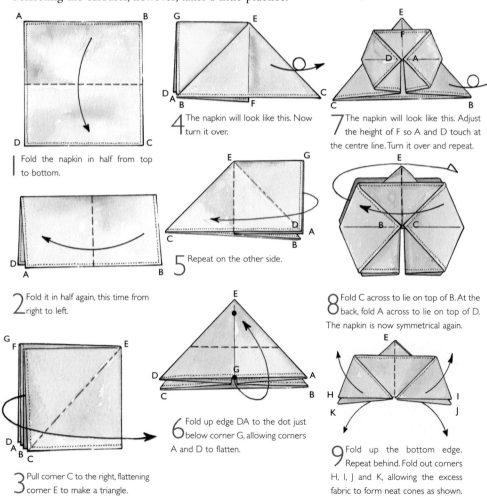

1 Fold the napkin in half from top to bottom.

2 Fold it in half again, this time from right to left.

3 Pull corner C to the right, flattening corner E to make a triangle.

4 The napkin will look like this. Now turn it over.

5 Repeat on the other side.

6 Fold up edge DA to the dot just below corner G, allowing corners A and D to flatten.

7 The napkin will look like this. Adjust the height of F so A and D touch at the centre line. Turn it over and repeat.

8 Fold C across to lie on top of B. At the back, fold A across to lie on top of D. The napkin is now symmetrical again.

9 Fold up the bottom edge. Repeat behind. Fold out corners H, I, J and K, allowing the excess fabric to form neat cones as shown.

the fan

This charming fold can be used for any occasion. Make it in white for the most formal; use coloured napkins for informal entertaining. This Fan is cleverly designed so that it sits up happily without support.

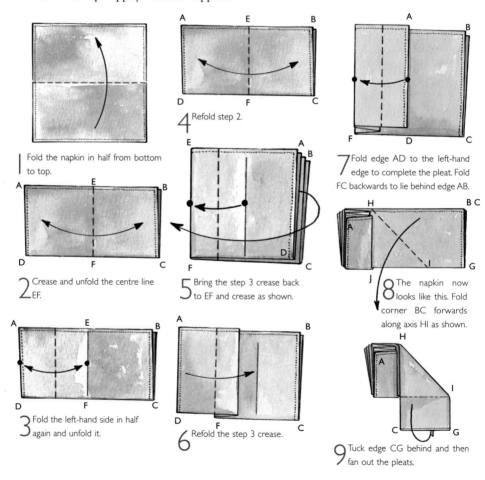

1 Fold the napkin in half from bottom to top.

2 Crease and unfold the centre line EF.

3 Fold the left-hand side in half again and unfold it.

4 Refold step 2.

5 Bring the step 3 crease back to EF and crease as shown.

6 Refold the step 3 crease.

7 Fold edge AD to the left-hand edge to complete the pleat. Fold FC backwards to lie behind edge AB.

8 The napkin now looks like this. Fold corner BC forwards along axis HI as shown.

9 Tuck edge CG behind and then fan out the pleats.

stitch directory

Couching

This a method for attaching either a thick thread or string, or group of threads, on to the surface of a fabric.

| Position the string on the fabric and as you hold it in place, take tiny stitches across the string using sewing thread to attach it to the fabric.

Cross stitch

This simple embroidery stitch is one of the oldest and most common.

| First, stitch a neat line of diagonal stitches, as shown.

2 Work back, completing each cross with a second diagonal stitch. Make sure the top half of each stitch slants in the same direction.

Daisy stitch

Also called 'lazy daisy stitch', this comprises a single chain stitch caught down with a small stitch at one end.

| Bring the needle up from the wrong side and make a loop. Pass the needle back down next to where you brought it up. Then bring the needle up about 1 cm/½in away, within the loop.

2 Make a straight stitch to anchor the loop, then bring the needle up at the point where you want to start the next petal. Repeat to create a circle of petals.

French knots

Used to add texture and colour, French knots can also fill a shape with shading.

| Bring the needle up from the wrong side and take a stitch. Twist the thread around the needle twice, pull through and take it back through next to the first hole. Finish off the knot.

Fly stitch

This stitch can be worked individually or in rows as a filling. Vary the length of the tail for different effects.

| Bring the needle up from the wrong side at the top left of the stitch. Insert the needle again at the top right-hand side of the stitch and bring it up at the bottom of the V.

2 Make a small stitch to anchor the bottom of the V, then bring the needle up at the top left of the next V to begin the next stitch.

Blanket stitch

This stitch was traditionally used to bind raw edges.

| Hold the material so the hem is at the top facing away from you. Bring the needle from the front and insert it upwards to the left, looping the thread below the needle. Pull the needle through and repeat.

Hem stitch

Hem stitch is used in drawn threadwork to group threads and finish the edge and hold the hem on the wrong side.

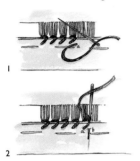

Bring the needle up at 'a', inside the hem. Pass it under four threads from right to left.

2 Take the needle down to the right behind the hem and bring it out at 'b'. Repeat to the end of the row.

Slip stitch

This is an almost invisible stitch used for joining two folded edges.

Bring a needle from the inside of one fold into the opposite fold.

2 Run the needle for a short way through the inside of the fold and then bring it out and into the opposite fold, through that fold, and so on.

Mitring a corner

This is a useful technique for neatening corners when making a hem.

Press under a narrow turning around the fabric, then press under the hem allowance. Unfold all the creases. Turn the corner over at 45 degrees so that the folds line up to form a square. Press the corner.

2 Unfold the corner and then trim it off, placing the cut a short distance from the angled crease.

3 Re-fold and press the creases, then tack (baste) the hem and mitred corner in place. Slip stitch the mitre together, working from the point inwards, then remove the tacks.

Turk's Head Knot

This knot can be tricky to perfect. Practise tying it on a length of cord.

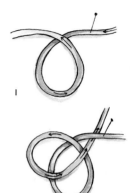

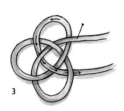

Measure a point 15cm/6in from one end of the cord. Pin it to a surface. Make a loop from right to left.

2 Make a second loop on top and to the left of the first. Pass the working end under the pinned end.

3 Loop the cord up to the left, over the top of the second loop, under the left side of the first, over the bottom of the second loop and under the right side of the first.

4 Draw up the three loops to form a ball, keeping the tension even and ensuring the cord is not twisted.

napkin folding symbols

Large, well-starched napkins always give the best results. If you don't have time for traditional starching, give your napkins a quick whoosh with spray starch before ironing. Napkin folding borrows most of its symbols from origami, most of which are self-explanatory. Here's the key:

Valley fold

A fold that has the effect of creating a valley of fabric, indicated in the book with a purple dotted line.

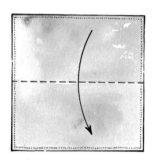

Existing crease

A fold that is already in place is shown by an unbroken line.

Fold dot to dot

Two black dots give precise positions for where the indicated fold should go. The dot at the bottom should lie on top of the dot by the arrow's point when the fold has been made.

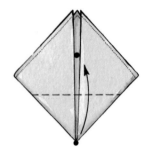

Mountain fold

A fold that creates a peak of fabric is shown with a green dotted line.

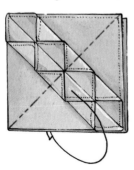

Turn over

A looped arrow indicates that the whole napkin should be turned round so that what was the back is now facing you.

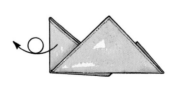

Backwards fold

When the arrow has only half a point, and is not filled in black, the fold should go behind the napkin.

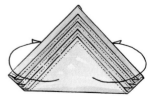

templates

The following template and motifs should be enlarged as necessary to suit the size of your napkin.

Hand-painted motif

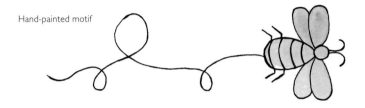 

Couched organdie

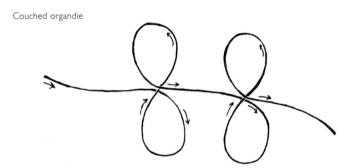 

Fretwork-style felt

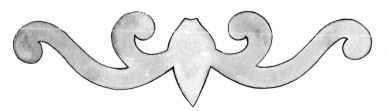 

index

anniversaries 20
antique effects 68

beach party 30–1
beaded rings 80
bee decorated napkin
 45
 template 143
bee on a wire ring 85
blanket stitch 140,
 edged napkin 39
blue settings 96–7
book, linen 71
bow ring, paper 63
buttoned wraps 56
buying napkins 7

cable fold 131
candle wax, removing 12
cards, holding 59
caring for napkins 12
carousel fold 136
celebrations 20
chevron fold 114
choosing napkins 7, 11
Christmas settings 99
clown's hat fold 123
cockscomb fold 117
cocktail party 26
concertina ring 63
corner, mitring 141
couched organdie 36
 couching 140
 template 143
couching 140
 organdie napkin 36
 template 143
cross stitch 140
 edged napkin 39, 41
cutlery roll 52

daisy stitch 140
 napkin edging 41

damask 11
decorated napkins 32–45
 couched organdie 36
 drawn threadwork 42
 edgings 38–9
 embroidery 39, 41
 hand-painted 45, 142
diamond fold 118
dining out 15
double swan fold 128
dragonfly wire ring 85
drawn threadwork 42

edgings 38–9
electrical wire rings 84–5
embroidery 39, 41
 drawn threadwork 42
 stitch directory 140–1
envelope fold 51

family lunch 22–3
fan fold 138
fan ring, paper 63
fasteners, frogging 66–7
felt rings 82
 template 143
festive theme 99
filigree beaded rings 80
flame fold 112
flower ring, beaded 80
flowers, holding 59
fly stitch 140
foil place tags 83
folding 48–9, 104–139
 antique-effect pockets 68–9
 buttoned wraps 56
 cable 131
 carousel 136
 chevrons 114
 clown's hat 123
 cockscomb 117
 diamond 118
 double swan 128
 envelope 51
 fan 138
 flame 112
 French lily 120
 lover's knot 124
 mitre 126
 opera house 135
 parcelled surprise 54
 slipper 132
 starfish 111
 symbols for 142
 wave 108
French knots 140
 napkin edging 41
French lily fold 120
fretwork felt rings 82
 template 143

frogged fasteners 66–7
 Turk's head knot 141

gold painted rings 78
green settings 94

hand-painting fabric 45
 template 143
hem stitch 141
history of napkins 10–11
holding and folding 46–71
 cards and flowers 59
 cutlery roll 52
 linen book 71
 organza sachets 60
 parcelled surprise 54
 pocket for storage 64

initial ring, beaded 80
ironing 12

lantern decoration, paper 76
laundering 12
layered paper ring 63
lover's knot fold 124
lunch 22–3

mitre fold 126
mitring a corner 141

napkin folds see
 folding
napkin rings see rings
nature-inspired settings 100

opera house fold 135
organdie, couched 36
 couching 140
 template 143
organza sachets 60
oriental settings 90

painted motif 45
 template 143
paper bow ring 63
paper fan ring 63
paper lantern
 decoration 76
paper star ring 76
parcelled surprise 54
picnic 29
place tags, foil 83
place cards, star 82
pocket, storage 64
 antique-effect 68–9
 see also frogged fasteners
pressing 12

red wine stains 12
ribbon and rick-rack trim 38

rick-rack and ribbon trim 38
rings, 72–85
 buttoned wraps 56
 concertina 63
 filigree beaded 80
 fine wirework 84–5
 foil place tags 83
 fretwork-style felt 82, 142
 gold painted 78
 layered paper 63
 paper bow 63
 paper fan 63
 paper star 76
 silver safety pin 79
running stitch edging 41

sachets, organza 60
scorch marks 12
seasonal settings 100
silver safety pin rings 79
size of napkins 11
slipper fold 132
spicy food stains 12
stains, removing 12
star place cards 82
starching 12
starfish fold 111
stitch directory 140–1
 see also embroidery
storing 12
 napkin pocket 64
summer picnic 29
supper party 24–5
symbols for folding 142

table decorations 76
templates 143
themed settings 86–103
 blue 96–97
 Christmas 99
 green 94
 nature 100
 oriental 90
 Victorian 102
 white 93
Turk's head knot 141
 frogged fasteners 66–7

using a napkin 15

Victorian settings 102

washing 12
wave fold 108
weddings 19
white settings 93
wirework rings 84–5
wraps, buttoned 56